MW00619992

PRIESTHOOD
POWER

PRIESTHOOD POWER

BLESSING THE SICK AND AFFLICTED

LARRY BARKDULL

Covenant Communications, Inc.

Cover image: Healing Hands © Adam Abram. For more information, visit www.olivewoodbooks.com

Cover design copyrighted 2008 by Covenant Communications, Inc.

Published by Covenant Communications, Inc.
American Fork, Utah

Printed in Canada
First Printing: November 2008

14 13 12 11 10 09 08   10 9 8 7 6 5 4 3 2 1

ISBN-13 978-1-59811-641-0
ISBN-10 1-59811-641-X

To Ted Gibbons, who honors the priesthood

The Church Handbook of Instructions, Book 2 contains the official Church statement regarding elders' responsibilities and procedures for administering to the sick and afflicted. This booklet, *Administering to the Sick and Afflicted,* contains information from a variety of sources, including the scriptures and General Authorities' statements, regarding this sacred ordinance. The author, editorial staff, and publisher have made every attempt to ensure accuracy. However, this booklet is not an official production of the Church, and any information herein is subordinate to the official Church materials on the subject. Any suggestions and interpretations are the author's, and the material in this booklet is simply intended to elevate priesthood holders' understanding and faith with regard to this important priesthood ordinance.

TABLE OF CONTENTS

CHAPTER 1
WE BELIEVE IN THE GIFT OF HEALING

"Is any sick among you? let him call for the elders of the church."[1] Our commission in the Melchizedek Priesthood is the same that Jesus gave to his Apostles when he sent them forth to serve: "Heal the sick, cleanse the lepers, raise the dead, cast out devils: freely ye have received, freely give."[2] That same authority with its commission has been restored to the earth. Elder Matthew Cowley related the following healing incident, demonstrating our commission:

> I was down on the Indian reservation when I met a sister who had just joined the Church, a beautiful Navajo woman . . . After I had met this sister, one of the missionaries called me off to the side and said, "A few months ago my companion and I went into a hogan and that lady, that Indian sister, was lying on the ground on a sheepskin. She had been lying there for six long years. We called on her, and when we were leaving she called us back and said in broken

1

English, 'Isn't there something you do for sick people?' And we said, 'Yes.' She said, 'Please do it for me.'" So they got down on their knees and administered to her, by the authority of the priesthood and in the name of Jesus Christ. Then they left, and they weren't away fifty yards when she came out of the hogan after them and said, "Come back and see what you have done for me." She walked.[3]

From the early days of the Restoration, this commandment to use the priesthood in such service has been observed. Oliver B. Huntington related this account of Joseph Smith:

Soon after Joseph settled in Kirtland, members of the Church began to gather to that place. The name of Joseph Smith and his power with God aroused everybody either for good or for bad. Mrs. John Johnson, who lived at the town of Hiram, forty miles distant from Kirtland, heard of the wonderful man that could receive revelations from God, heal the sick and see angels. She had a stiff arm that she wanted healed and made useful like the other, so she induced her husband to take a journey to Kirtland to see the Prophet.

Joseph asked her if she believed that God could make him instrumental in healing her arm which had been stiff a long time.

She answered that she believed her arm could be healed. The Prophet only remarked that he would visit her the next day. The next day Joseph came to Bishop Newell K. Whitney's home where Mr. Johnson and his wife were staying. There were a Campbellite doctor and a Methodist preacher in the room. [Joseph] took Mrs. Johnson by the hand and without sitting down or standing on ceremonies, and after a very short mental prayer, pronounced her arm whole in the name of Jesus Christ. He left the house immediately.

When he was gone, the preacher asked if her arm was well. She immediately stretched out her arm straight, remarking at the same time, "It's as well as the other."[4]

Elder Bruce R. McConkie wrote, "Ordinances of administration with actual healings resulting therefrom are one of the evidences of the divinity of the Lord's work."[5] This was true of both the Restored Church and the ancient Church; healing the sick was an essential part of Jesus' ministry. "And Jesus went about all Galilee, teaching in their synagogues, and preaching the gospel of the kingdom, and healing all manner of sickness and all manner of disease among the people . . . and they brought unto him all sick people that were taken with divers diseases and torments, and those which were possessed with devils, and those which were lunatick, and those that had the palsy; and he healed them."[6] Clearly, there was no affliction that did not yield when it encountered the Lord's command. As representatives of Jesus Christ, we are commissioned to do the work of Christ.

As noted, the Prophet Joseph Smith set the latter-day example for the Saints. After being expelled from Missouri, the Saints were huddled in Illinois when cholera struck their camp. Soon the devastating sickness had enveloped the Saints and death began sweeping through their ranks. The Prophet deeply pondered the situation then acted. Wilford Woodruff wrote the following account:

> On the morning of the 22nd of July, 1839, [the Prophet] arose reflecting upon the situation of the Saints of God in their persecutions and afflictions. He called upon the Lord in prayer, and the power of God rested mightily upon him. And as Jesus healed all the sick around Him in His day, so Joseph, the Prophet of God, healed all around on this occasion. He healed all in his house and dooryard, then, in company with Sidney Rigdon and several of the Twelve, he went through among the sick lying on the bank of the river, and he commanded

them in a loud voice, in the name of Jesus Christ, to come up and be made whole, and they were all healed. . . .

[After healing those on the east side of the river, they crossed over and healed others.] I felt the power of God that was overwhelming His prophet. When we entered the house, Brother Joseph walked up to Brother Fordham and took him by the right hand; in his left hand he held his hat.

He saw that Brother Fordham's eyes were glazed, and that he was speechless and unconscious.

After taking hold of his hand, the Prophet looked down into the dying man's face and said, "Brother Fordham, do you not know me?" . . .

With a low whisper, Brother Fordham [finally] answered, "Yes."

The Prophet then said, "Have you not faith to be healed?"

The answer, which was a little plainer than before, was, "I am afraid it is too late. If you had come sooner, I think I might have been." . . .

Joseph then said, "Do you believe that Jesus is the Christ?"

"I do, Brother Joseph," was the response.

Then the Prophet of God spoke with a loud voice, as in the majesty of the Godhead, "Elijah, I command you, in the name of Jesus of Nazareth, to arise and be made whole!"

The words of the Prophet were not like the words of man, but like the voice of God. It seemed to me that the house shook from its foundation. Elijah Fordham leaped from his bed like a man raised from the dead. A healthy color came to his face, and life was manifested in every act. His feet were done up in Indian-meal poultices. He kicked them off his feet, scattered the contents, then called for his clothes and put them on. He asked for a bowl of bread and milk and ate it. Then he put on his hat and followed us into the street to visit others who were sick.[7]

The account continues with story after miraculous story of the Prophet—and those he gave assignment to—healing many, as well as casting out evil spirits among those who came to stop the work of God. Clearly, from this account, we believe in the gift of healing and the gift of faith and its role in the healing process.

CHAPTER 2
WHAT IS A PRIESTHOOD
ORDINANCE?

Administering to the sick and afflicted is a priesthood *ordinance*.[8] Priesthood blessings of direction, comfort, and counsel are not listed in the *Church Handbook of Instructions* as ordinances but rather as "Father's Blessings and Other Blessings of Comfort and Counsel," which are performed in a different manner.[9] This distinction should signal the singular and sacred purpose of the administration ordinance. Explaining ordinances, Elder Bruce R. McConkie wrote:

> God's decrees, his laws and command-
> ments, the statutes and judgments that
> issue from him, are called his ordinances.
> . . . Among his laws and commandments,
> the Lord has provided certain rites and
> ceremonies which are also called ordi-
> nances. These ordinance-rites might be
> pictured as a small circle within the larger
> circle of ordinance-commandments.
> Most of these rites and ceremonies, as
> illustrated by baptism and celestial
> marriage, are essential to salvation and

exaltation in the kingdom of God; some
of them, such as the blessing of children
and the dedication of graves, are not
ordinances of salvation, but are performed for the comfort, consolation,
and encouragement of the saints.[10]

An ordinance is typically comprised of authoritative
words, rich symbolic actions, and/or physical tokens,
which, by means of a physical action, are intended to
help draw the mind toward sacred, spiritual things.[11] All
of these are integrated into the ordinance of healing the
sick.

In addition to the significance of the acts accompanying the ordinance, the word *ordinance* itself is important in directing our minds toward God.

The word "ordinance" is derived from
the Latin *ordinare,* which means to put
in order or sequence; or to act by
authorization or command. . . .
Religious ordinances [are not] arbitrari-
ly established but [are] purposefully
instituted by God and eternal in scope.

The power to perform ordinances
whose validity is recognized by God is
inseparably connected with . . . the
priesthood of God. . . . When ordinances are performed with authority
and power, they are followed by divine
blessings. They have "efficacy, virtue,
[and] force" (D&C 132:7). They are

enlightening to the mind and enlivening to the whole soul (JS—H 1:74). The first man, after he entered the process of baptism, was "quickened in the inner man" (Moses 6:65). Ordinances unify man with God, and man with man: "Behold, thou art one in me, a son of God; and thus may all become my sons" (Moses 6:68).[12]

Priesthood ordinances are broadly divided into two categories: 1) *essential for salvation,* and 2) *non-essential for salvation.* For example, "some ordinances are prerequisite for entering celestial glory (baptism, gift of the Holy Ghost) and for exaltation (priesthood ordination, temple Endowment, celestial marriage),"[13] while other ordinances such as the naming and blessing of children, dedication of graves, and the consecrating of oil are *non-salvation-essential* ordinances. Administering to the sick and afflicted is a *non-salvation-essential* priesthood ordinance. All ordinances are for the purpose of blessing God's children, and because they are performed in the name of Jesus Christ and by His authority, they are recognized as valid in both heaven and on earth.

The administration ordinance is often misunderstood. Because we elders are not given set words to pronounce in administration blessings, we must seek to draw upon the inspiration of the Spirit for guidance. This can (and should) cause us deep reflection and humility. Whereas we never question the validity of ordinances such as baptism, priesthood ordination, or temple marriage, we sometimes stumble when it comes to administrations.

Consequently, we may approach the ordinance with questions and doubts rather than faith. Spoken or unspoken, doubt and fear tend to drive away the Spirit, and the recipient, who has requested the blessing because of his urgent need, may be left to himself to try to increase his faith. Simply put, if the Lord's servants have limited faith in the power of the priesthood, how can a recipient exercise faith in that power?

While it is true that all administrations are subject to the will of God (Paul was left with a "thorn in the flesh"[14] perhaps for a good purpose[15]), our commission remains the same: we are to live worthily so we can effectively seek the Spirit in a person's behalf, then confidently and authoritatively minister in the Lord's name. As much as we must not step ahead of the Lord and put words in His mouth, we also must not make excuses for Him. When we are called upon, we must with humble assurance perform the administration ordinance correctly, then leave the timing and specifics up to the Lord. We are servants *of* the Lord; we are not *the* Lord. After we have performed the ordinance and pronounced the blessing, we have no more ability to effect its realization than a patriarch has the ability to effect the promises given in a patriarchal blessing. Once any priesthood blessing is given, it belongs to the recipient, who then shoulders the entire responsibility to work out the details of his blessing with the Lord.

Administration—An Ordinance with a Specific Purpose

Priesthood ordinances are performed for specific purposes. The administration ordinance has a single purpose: to heal the sick and afflicted, unless the recipient is appointed unto death. "And the elders of the church, two or more, shall be called, and shall *pray for* and *lay their hands* upon them *in my name*; and if they die they shall die unto me, and if they live they shall live unto me. . . . And again, it shall come to pass that he that hath *faith in me to be healed,* and is not appointed unto death, *shall be healed.*"[16]

Of course, the Lord understands that there are many levels of faith that can result in varieties of and timetables for healings. If a person does not have the faith to be healed promptly, or if the Lord chooses to allow the condition to linger as part of His "purposeful plan,"[17] we believe that the administration, coupled with nurturing, will comfort, eventually heal, or at least improve the recipient's condition. "And whosoever among you are sick, and have not faith to be healed, but believe, shall be nourished with all tenderness, with herbs and mild food, and that not by the hand of an enemy."[18]

Nevertheless, we must remember that the Lord has unequivocally stated that the purpose of this ordinance is to heal the sick and afflicted—exempting those who are appointed unto death. Elder Bruce R. McConkie writes, "[The recipient] shall be healed unless he is appointed unto death."[19] Notwithstanding, the administration ordinance functions by faith and according to the Lord's thoughts and ways.[20] The revelation in D&C 42 continues with repeats of the two qualifiers—faith and appointment to death—and the Lord's promise: "And again, it shall come to pass that he that hath faith in me to be healed, and is not appointed unto death, *shall be healed.* He who hath faith to see *shall see.* He who hath faith to hear *shall hear.* The lame who hath faith to leap *shall leap.*"[21]

Clearly, if we doubt the purpose, use, or criteria of the administration ordinance, we are mistaken and lack faith in the ordinance. But also clearly, the Lord can employ whatever means and time frame He chooses to determine or effect the healing. Implied or spoken, every blessing should contain the phrase of submission: "Nevertheless not my will, but thine, be done."[22] Our responsibility is to recognize that the administration is a priesthood ordinance with a specific purpose and performed in a singular way; therefore, we must consider it as effective as any other ordinance of the Holy Priesthood.

CHAPTER 3
DO WE REALLY BELIEVE IN JESUS CHRIST AND HIS POWER?

The Melchizedek Priesthood is the Holy Priesthood, after the order of the Son of God.[23] To hold the high priesthood suggests that we have a testimony of the reality of Jesus Christ. Alma taught that we, who qualify to hold the priesthood here on earth, had premortally (in that "first place"[24]) "conformed to the image of [God's] Son."[25] That is, we loved the work of redemption in the premortal world and thereby distinguished ourselves to receive the high priesthood in mortality. Having been "called and prepared from the foundation of the world . . . on account of [our] exceeding faith and good works,"[26] we now become lights or types of Jesus Christ that through our lives we might show God's children "what manner to look forward to his Son for redemption."[27]

According to President J. Reuben Clark, we, who hold the Melchizedek Priesthood, are of that group that Abraham called

> "The noble and great ones." . . .
> Following upon this general principle, the Prophet Joseph said: "Every man who has a calling," *every man,* "to minister to the

13

inhabitants of the world was ordained to that very purpose in the grand council of heaven before this world was." . . . I do not know whether we have a right to interpret the Prophet's statement, . . . but I like to think that it does include those of us of lesser calling and lesser stature. We have been told ever since I was old enough to remember that those who are coming forth among the Latter-day Saints were choice spirits, and I like to think that perhaps in that grand council something at least was said to us indicating what would be expected of us, and empowering us, subject to the re-confirmation here, to do certain things in building up the kingdom of God on earth.[28]

Our priesthood calling in mortality indicates that we believed and believe in Jesus Christ; we have always believed in Him and His power. And our obligation, given that belief, is to build His kingdom on earth. "To build up the kingdom of God," as President Clark said, is to bless God's children, and blessing God's children can only take place by and through the authority of and faith in Jesus Christ. In *Lectures on Faith,* Joseph Smith taught that faith in Jesus Christ is built on the following foundation[29]:

1. Faith that He actually exists.
We often skip over this criterion and move on to the next, because it seems so obvious. But consider this:

when an urgent situation invades our lives, we always review our testimony to re-verify our belief that the Lord truly lives. If we harbor the slightest doubt of the Lord's reality, our faith is weakened as we attempt to act in His name.

2. Faith in His perfections, characteristics, and attributes.

That the Lord exists leads to the question *What is He like?* Jesus Christ is like God the Father in every way. They are perfect beings who are not progressing to develop moral attributes of character. The Prophet Joseph Smith listed their perfections as 1) *Characteristics:* everlasting, merciful, gracious, slow to anger, abundant in goodness, unchangeable, [Gods] of truth that cannot lie, no respecters of persons (show no favoritism), [Gods] of love;[30] 2) *Attributes:* total knowledge of everything (past, present, and future), total power, total justice, total judgment, total mercy, and total truth.[31]

3. Faith that we are worthy before God.

Although a man may be ordained to the priesthood and be given the *authority* to act in the Lord's name, that man only gains the *power* of the priesthood through righteous living.[32] When called upon to act in the Lord's name and bless His children, a priesthood holder might go to his knees and ask the Lord to search him for worthiness (although we would expect that this is an ongoing process). The Holy Ghost seems to quickly respond to the question: *What do I need to repent of?* Why would the Holy Ghost not be anxious to answer such prayers, assuming that they are offered with "real intent"?[33] A good measurement of a man's worthiness is his ability to honestly answer the temple recommend questions and constantly try to mirror God's attributes and characteristics. We might take King Benjamin's teachings as a guide for increasing our faith through worthiness: "[A priesthood holder] yields to the enticings of the Holy Spirit, and putteth off the natural man and becometh a saint through the atonement of Christ the Lord, and becometh as a child, submissive, meek, humble, patient, full of love, willing to submit to all things which the Lord seeth fit to inflict upon him, even as a child doth submit to his father."[34]

The Power of the *Words of God*

There is a vast difference between the way man works and God works. To accomplish most things, man must exert physical effort; God, on the other hand, works by faith[35] and the power of words. The Nephite prophet Jacob said, "For behold, by the *power of his word* man came upon the face of the earth, which earth was created by the *power of his word.* Wherefore, if God being able to *speak* and the world was, and to *speak* and man was created, O then, why not able to command the earth, or the workmanship of his hands upon the face of it, according to his will and pleasure?"[36] Clearly, God works by faith and the power of words.

The word of God is the language of the priesthood, therefore the word of God is sure. It never fails. "What I the Lord have spoken, I have spoken, and I excuse not myself; and though the heavens and the earth pass away, *my word shall not pass away, but shall all be fulfilled,* whether by mine own voice or by the voice of my servants, it is the same."[37] In salvation-essential ordinances, those who hold the priesthood are authorized to speak the word of God, and those actions are recorded both on earth and in heaven.[38] Then, if the person who receives the ordinance remains worthy, those words of God spoken in the ordinance will never fail. In the non-salvation-essential ordinances, such as administrations, the Holy Spirit dictates the word of God. If, in such ordinances, priesthood holders speak the word of God as dictated by the Holy Spirit in faith, and if, in faith, the recipient receives the word of God and lives worthily, those inspired words are likewise valid. Therefore, we must act in righteousness and with full and complete faith that we are annunciating the word of God as the Spirit communicates it to us. Then, subject to the qualified conditions listed herein, the words that we speak "shall not pass away, but shall all be fulfilled."[39]

In *Lectures on Faith,* Joseph Smith taught about the power of the word of God:

> We understand that when a man works by faith, he works by *mental exertion* instead of physical force. It is *by words,* instead of exerting his physical powers, with which every being works when he works by faith. God said, "Let there be light: and there was light" [Gen. 1:3]. Joshua spake, and the great lights which God had created stood still [Josh. 10:12–13]. Elijah commanded, and the heavens were stayed for the space of three years and six months, so that it did not rain: he again commanded and the

heavens gave forth rain [1 Kgs. 17:1; 18:1, 41–45]. All this was done by faith. And the Saviour says, "If you have faith as a grain of mustard seed, say to this mountain, 'Remove' . . . and it will remove; or say unto that sycamine tree, 'Be ye plucked up . . . and . . . planted in the sea' and it shall obey you" [Matt. 17:20, Luke 17:6]. *Faith, then, works by words; and with these its mightiest works have been, and will be, performed.*[40]

Enoch learned and spoke the word of God by which he performed mighty miracles:

And so great was the faith of Enoch that he led the people of God, and their enemies came to battle against them; *and he spake the word of the Lord,* and the earth trembled, and the mountains fled, even according to his command; and the rivers of water were turned out of their course; and the roar of the lions was heard out of the wilderness; and all nations feared greatly, *so powerful was the word of Enoch, and so great was the power of the language which God had given him.*[41]

Other prophets have testified of the power of the word of God:
• Paul: "Through faith we understand that the worlds were framed *by the word of God,* so that things which

are seen were not made of things which do appear."[42]

- Moroni: "Who shall say that it was not a miracle that *by his word* the heaven and the earth should be; and *by the power of his word* man was created of the dust of the earth; and *by the power of his word* have miracles been wrought?"[43]

- Nephi: "Now ye know that Moses was commanded of the Lord to do that great work; and ye know that *by his word* the waters of the Red Sea were divided hither and thither, and they passed through on dry ground."[44]

The Power of the Name of Jesus Christ—The *Word of God*

The *words of God* flow from the *Word* or the *Word of Power* or the *Word of God*—all names for Jesus Christ. Moses learned that Jesus, the *Word of God*, is the foundation upon which are built the *words of God*: "And [Moses] beheld many lands; and each land was called earth, and there were inhabitants on the face thereof. And it came to pass that Moses called upon God, saying: Tell me, I pray thee, why these things are so, and by what thou madest them? . . . [God answered,] And by *the word of my power*, have I created them, which is mine Only Begotten Son, who is full of grace and truth."[45]

Clearly, the "words of God" emanate from the "Word of God." Jesus Christ is both a person and the universal "Word"[46] of authority and power. Elders are authorized to use this "Word"—*Jesus Christ*—to speak the "words of God" by means of blessings and ordinances. The Lord explained that the power to become

Godly is manifested by means of priesthood ordinances: "And this greater priesthood administereth the gospel and holdeth the key of the mysteries of the kingdom, even the key of the knowledge of God. *Therefore, in the ordinances thereof, the power of godliness is manifest. And without the ordinances thereof, and the authority of the priesthood, the power of godliness is not manifest unto men in the flesh.*"[47] When a man has the Melchizedek Priesthood conferred upon him, he has the name of *Jesus Christ* "put upon him" so that he may represent the Lord and speak the *words of God* by use of *His name.* The Lord explained to Abraham, "Behold, I will lead thee by my hand, and I will take thee, *to put upon thee my name, even the Priesthood.*"[48]

The power of the name of Jesus Christ is unequaled. During His mortal ministry, Jesus ordained the Seventy, gave them power to use His name, then sent them on missions, part of which was to perform administrations as a sign that the representatives of the kingdom of heaven had come to the people. He instructed the Seventy, "Heal the sick . . . therein, and say unto them, The kingdom of heaven is come nigh unto you [i.e. *We have come with power as authorized servants from the kingdom of heaven and have authority to use the name of Jesus Christ to bless you*]."[49] When the Seventy returned from their missions, they were astonished at the power of the name of Jesus Christ: "And the seventy returned again with joy, saying, Lord, even the devils are subject unto us *through thy name.*"[50]

Through the ordinance of baptism we first receive the name of *Jesus Christ;* through the ordinance of confirmation we are *adopted* into Jesus' family.[51] But having

a new family name—*Jesus Christ*—and a new family—
The Church of Jesus Christ of Latter-day Saints—does not
mean that we have the authority to use the name of Jesus
Christ to speak for and act in the Lord's place. Priesthood
is required for that. Therefore, when a man worthily
qualifies to receive the priesthood, he has conferred upon
him the authority to use the name of his *adopted* father,
Jesus Christ, to bless the members of the family of Jesus
Christ, and also to bless other people who are not yet
members of that family. An elder also receives the authority to invite other people into the family of Jesus Christ.

Concerning the importance of the name of Jesus
Christ, the Lord commands us to "take upon you *the
name of Christ* . . . Behold, *Jesus Christ is the name* which
is given of the Father, and there is none other name given
whereby man can be saved [now or in the future] . . . for
in that name [Jesus Christ] shall they be called at the last
day."52

Miracles Follow Faith

Do we really believe in the power of the priesthood? Do
we believe what Moses said?

> Every one being ordained after this
> order and calling should have power, by
> faith, to break mountains, to divide the
> seas, to dry up waters, to turn them out
> of their course;
>
> To put at defiance the armies of
> nations, to divide the earth, to break
> every band, to stand in the presence of
> God; to do all things according to his

will, according to his command, subdue principalities and powers; and this by the will of the Son of God which was from before the foundation of the world.[53]

A careful reading of the Lord's injunction to His Nephite disciples suggests that signs and miracles follow or attend elders who truly believe: "And these signs shall follow them [elders] that believe—in my name shall they [elders] cast out devils; they [elders] shall speak with new tongues; they [elders] shall take up serpents; and if they [elders] drink any deadly thing it shall not hurt them; *they [elders] shall lay hands on the sick and they [the recipients] shall recover.*"[54] Then the Lord offered His disciples the following words of comfort, which, when considered from an elder's point of view, should increase the elder's faith and give him courage to act in the Lord's name: "And whosoever [an elder] shall believe in my name, doubting nothing, unto him [an elder] will I confirm all my words, even unto the ends of the earth."[55] In other words, when we are on the Lord's errand, He will not let us fall; He will confirm the words that we speak in His name "unto the ends of the earth."

President Brigham Young declared his faith in the ability of the Lord's servants to heal through the Lord's name and power:

> When I lay hands on the sick, I expect the healing power and influence of God to pass through me to the patient, and the disease to give way. I do not say that

I heal everybody I lay hands on; but many have been healed under my administration. . . . When we are prepared, when we are holy vessels before the Lord, a stream of power from the Almighty can pass though the tabernacle of the administrator to the system of the patient, and the sick are made whole; the headache, fever or other disease has to give way.[56]

CHAPTER 4
PREPARING TO REPRESENT JESUS CHRIST

Would anyone presume to speak in the name of Jesus Christ without first sanctifying himself by repenting, humbly and adequately preparing, and trying to become like Jesus Christ in every way? Otherwise, casual behavior might qualify as taking the name of God in vain.[57]

> Wherefore, let all men beware how they take my name in their lips—
>
> For behold, verily I say, that many there be who are under this condemnation, who use the name of the Lord, and use it in vain, having not authority. . . .
>
> Remember that that which cometh from above is sacred, and must be spoken with care, and by constraint of the Spirit; and in this there is no condemnation, and ye receive the Spirit through prayer wherefore, without this there remaineth condemnation.[58]

Personal Sanctification

Joseph Smith explained the importance of personal sanctification [both for elders and recipients] so that miracles might follow. "I spoke, and admonished the members of the Church individually to set their houses in order, to make clean the inside of the platter, and to meet on the next Sabbath to partake of the Sacrament, in order that by our obedience to the ordinances, we might be enabled to prevail with God against the destroyer, and that the sick might be healed."[59] Then, when the Saints heeded his counsel, the promised blessings flowed. The Prophet wrote, "This week I spent chiefly among the sick. . . . sickness decreasing."[60]

The Nephite prophet Jacob described the result of sanctifying preparation so that we might better use the name of Jesus Christ to speak the *words of God*: "Wherefore, we search the prophets, and we have many revelations and the spirit of prophecy; and having all these witnesses we obtain a hope, and our faith becometh unshaken, insomuch that *we truly can command in the name of Jesus* and the very trees obey us, or the mountains, or the waves of the sea."[61]

Jacob explained that power in the priesthood comes by searching "the prophets," that is, by searching the scriptures. By so doing, we become familiar with the voice of the Spirit, we enjoy "many revelations," and we develop the "spirit of prophecy," which is the "testimony of Jesus" (Revelation 19:10). Jacob stated that "all these witnesses" from the Spirit increase our hope, faith, and spiritual experience, until our confidence in Jesus Christ and His name become "unshaken," and we truly can perform many mighty miracles. Again we notice that a central criterion for using the name of Jesus Christ, to exercise His power effectively, is profound humility.

Then Jacob reminded us that the priesthood is ultimately the Lord's power, not man's power. Therefore, we humbly acknowledge our total inability to heal without His help; we humbly acknowledge that all divine manifestations of the power of God are linked to His goodness: "Nevertheless, the Lord God showeth us our weakness that we may know that *it is by his grace, and his great condescensions unto the children of men, that we have power to do these things.*"[62] Without humility and without the Lord's grace and condescension, we can do nothing.

Suggestions for Preparing to Give a Blessing

Here are some ideas for humble preparation:

- Pray for the gift of healing. We are commanded to earnestly seek the best spiritual gifts, among which is the "faith to heal."[63]

- Fast, if we have time, even for a short period. We are taught that fasting and prayer can assist a priesthood holder to more effectively administer to the sick.[64] Fasting infuses us with power: "to undo heavy burdens, and to let the oppressed go free . . . [to] break every yoke . . . Then thou shalt call, and the Lord shall answer; thou shalt cry, and he shall say, Here I am . . . and thou shalt be called, The repairer of the breach [one who fixes that which is broken]."[65]

- Read the scriptures to invite and become familiar and conversant with the voice of the Spirit.

- Attend the temple, if we have the time, before administering to the sick.

- Dress in Sunday clothes, i.e. dress shirt, tie, etc. How we appear suggests Whom we represent. Changing into Sunday clothes takes only a few minutes, but it sends a powerful message. Effectively, we are conveying to the recipient, "We are taking this ordinance seriously. We are prepared. We reverently acknowledge Whose servant we are and Whose name we bear." We are saying, as did the disciples of old, "The kingdom of God is come nigh unto you."[66] A priesthood holder who will take the time to dress in his best to administer this sacred ordinance will exemplify the dignity of his office, and the recipient might more readily feel that something of great and sacred importance is about to happen. Remember: healing only occurs by faith. Often, dressing nobly raises both our faith and the recipient's faith.

Elder Matthew Cowley supports several items on the above list. He said:

> Sometimes I wonder if we do enough in our administration of the sick. You know when the Apostles tried to cast out an evil spirit they couldn't do it. . . . The Master came along, and he immediately cast out the dumb spirit. Then the Apostles said, "Why could not we cast him out?" And what did Christ say? "This kind goeth not out but by prayer and by fasting." [see Matt. 17:21] . . . A little over a year ago a couple came into

my office carrying a little boy. The father said to me. "My wife and I have been fasting for two days, and we've brought our little boy up for a blessing. You are the one we've been sent to." . . . They said he was born blind, deaf and dumb, [had] no coordination of his muscles, [and] couldn't even crawl at the age of five years. I said to myself, "This is it." [*This kind goeth not out but by prayer and by fasting.*] . . . I blessed that child, and a few weeks later I received a letter: "Brother Cowley, we wish you could see our little boy now. He's crawling. When we throw a ball across the floor, he races after it on his hands and knees. He can see. When we clap our hands over his head, he jumps. He can hear." Medical science had laid the burden down. God had taken over.[67]

Becoming the Hands, Arms, and Voice of Jesus Christ
Concerning elders as representatives of Jesus Christ, Elder Bruce R. McConkie wrote, "As the Lord's agents, they pray and minister in the place and stead of their Master."[68] When we receive the Melchizedek Priesthood, we receive it with an oath and a covenant,[69] parts of which are to fully receive Jesus Christ [His atonement and His name] and to magnify our calling. Our *calling* includes our commission to bless the lives of others, which involves administering to the sick and afflicted.

Hence the charge: "Lay your hands upon the sick, and they shall recover."[70]

When we lay our hands upon the heads of the sick or afflicted, we become, in essence, the hands of Jesus Christ. For example, Edward Partridge was told by the Lord, "And I will lay *my hand* upon you *by the hand of my servant* Sidney Rigdon."[71] In a similar manner, priesthood holders are the arms of Jesus Christ: "And their arm shall be my arm."[72]

At another time, the Lord emphasized His willingness to support His servants when they, through the priesthood, minister in His name and thus become His voice: "What I the Lord have spoken, I have spoken, and I excuse not myself; and though the heavens and the earth pass away, my word shall not pass away, but shall all be fulfilled, *whether by mine own voice or by the voice of my servants, it is the same.*"[73]

Speaking to the subject of our representing the Lord, President Joseph Fielding Smith said, "We are ambassadors of the Lord Jesus Christ. Our commission is to represent him. We are directed to preach his gospel, to perform the ordinances of salvation, to bless mankind, to heal the sick and perhaps perform miracles, to do what he would do if he were personally present—and all this because we hold the holy priesthood."[74] And, as President Howard W. Hunter reminded us, "whatever Jesus lays his hands upon lives."[75]

Melchizedek Priesthood holders should become familiar with the procedure for administering to the sick and afflicted. The *Church Handbook of Instructions, Book 2,* pages 172–73 contains the Church's official instructions for all priesthood blessings. Please consult your

local priesthood leaders if you have questions from study-
ing the material herein.

CHAPTER 5
INVOKING THE LAW OF ASKING

Asking to receive could be considered a law of heaven. "Ask, and ye shall receive; knock, and it shall be opened unto you."[76] *Asking* is a manifestation of faith, and faith is required for healing. But with regard to asking, we elders should ask first before we encourage the recipient to ask.

Increasing *Our* Faith by Asking
We should ask in faith for the permission and power to heal: "The rights of the priesthood are inseparably connected with the powers of heaven."[77] Remember, healings are dependent upon faith (the recipient's and ours), therefore, we might ask for the gift of faith.[78]

As we have learned, *asking* is a manifestation of faith. We ask because we know that Jesus Christ lives; we ask because we are confident in His characteristics, attributes and perfections; we ask because we believe we are worthy to ask; and we ask because the Lord has promised to give liberally when we ask. "Ask, and ye *shall* receive"[79] is a commandment with a promise. In prefacing His revelation on the gifts of the Spirit (D&C 46), which includes the gift of healing, the Lord commanded and promised, "But ye are commanded in all things to ask of God, who giveth liberally"[80] and we are to "seek [ie., ask for] . . . earnestly the best gifts, always remembering for what they are given."[81] Clearly, we must ask for the gift of healing rather than assume we have it. The Lord gives an amazing promise to those who ask in faith for the gift of healing and who then are willing to go forth in confidence and perform administrations in His name: "For I am God, and mine arm is not shortened; and I *will* show miracles, signs, and wonders, unto all those who believe on my name. *And whoso shall ask it in my name in faith,* they *shall* cast out devils; they *shall* heal the sick; they *shall* cause the blind to receive their sight, and the deaf to hear, and the dumb to speak, and the lame to walk."[82]

The Recipient Should *Ask* to Be Blessed

Because *receiving* follows *asking,* the recipient should, if he is willing or capable, ask to receive a blessing. If he is not willing or capable, a family member, friend, or the elders should ask. In either case, because asking to receive is a law of God, someone should ask.

We ask because we trust that the Lord loves and hears and has the power to help us. "And this is the confidence that we have in him, that, if we ask any thing according to his will, he heareth us: And if we know that he hear us, whatsoever we ask, we know that we have the petitions that we desired of him."[83] Moreover, we ask because we believe that the Lord is merciful and has the power to help us: "Thou are merciful, thou wilt not suffer those who come unto thee that they shall perish!"[84]

In Jesus' day, some friends of a man with palsy carried him to the Lord for healing. Evidently, the man was too sick to ask for himself, so his friends, by their faith-filled actions, asked for him.[85] Jairus asked for his daughter, who was lying on her bed at the point of death.[86] A centurian beseeched Jesus in behalf of his servant.[87] Because someone must ask in faith, preferably the recipient, the Lord instructed: "Require not miracles, except I shall command you, *except* casting out devils, healing the sick, and against poisonous serpents, and against deadly poisons [for these situations we may ask the Lord for a miracle]; *And these things ye shall not do, except it be required of you by them who desire it,* that the scriptures might be fulfilled; for ye shall do according to that which is written."[88] That is, because the recipient recognizes in us the power of God, he, or someone close to him, is motivated by hope to ask us to use our power to perform an administration to heal him. His asking is a testimony of faith in God and His servants.

Helping to Increase the Recipient's Faith to Ask in Faith
We are often called upon to help increase the recipient's faith so that he can ask the Lord to bless him. Again, because healings are an outgrowth of the recipient's *faith* and *asking,* we, the representatives of the Lord, are in a unique position to help the recipient in this regard, especially when it comes to helping him verbalize his request. Jesus was the perfect example. On one occasion, the Savior urged the suffering father of a lunatic child to recommit to his testimony and raise his sights: "If thou canst believe, all things are possible to him that believeth. And straightway the father of the child cried out, and said with tears, Lord, I believe; help thou mine unbelief."[89] The cry of the father was a cry of faith, which proved sufficient for the Lord to bless his child as he had asked.

Another way that the Lord increased recipients' faith was by asking them questions to determine their level of faith:

> And when Jesus departed thence, two blind men followed him, crying, and saying, Thou Son of David, have mercy on us.
>
> And when he was come into the house, the blind men came to him: and Jesus saith unto them, Believe ye that I am able to do this? They said unto him, Yea, Lord.
>
> Then touched he their eyes, saying, According to your faith be it unto you.
>
> And their eyes were opened.[90]

When Jesus perceived that the level of their faith was sufficient to produce healing, He blessed them as they had asked.

Faith

President Spencer W. Kimball said:

> The need of faith is often underestimated. The ill one and the family often seem to depend wholly on the power of the priesthood and the gift of healing that they hope the administering brethren may have, whereas the greater responsibility is with him who is blessed[;] . . . the major element is the

faith of the individual when that person is conscious and accountable. "Thy faith hath made thee whole" was repeated so often by the Master that it almost became a chorus. Though he was the Redeemer and "all power [was] given [him] in heaven and in earth," yet his oft-repeated statement was, *"Thy faith hath made thee whole."* "As with your faith, so shall it be unto you."[91]

Helping to increase the recipient's faith to ask by the "prayer of faith."

Asking in faith to receive a blessing could be called the *prayer of faith.* Speaking of the importance of the prayer of faith, which precedes the administration, President Spencer W. Kimball also noted, "Then there is the *prayer that is unlike the administration*; it makes request to the Lord to heal and may be offered by any soul who has a desire to do so[,] and is not an ordinance in the same sense. The prayer is a request for the Lord to act, whereas the blessing or the administration is given by the brethren in the name of Christ."[92]

In emphasizing the prayer of faith's importance— either by the recipient, a friend, a loved one, or the elders— James, the brother of Jesus, wrote the following instructions:

> Is any sick among you? let him call for the elders of the church; and *let them pray over him*, anointing him with oil in the name of the Lord:

> *And the prayer of faith shall save the sick,* and the Lord shall raise him up; and if he have committed sins, they shall be forgiven him.
>
> Confess your faults one to another, *and pray one for another, that ye may be healed. The effectual fervent prayer of a righteous man availeth much.*[93]

While the "prayer of faith" noted above may indicate the elders' praying over the sick person in the attitude of anointing and blessing him, it may also indicate the prayer of faith that precedes the administration. James states that the more humble and righteous the requester is the greater will be his faith and the greater will be faith's power—"the effectual fervent prayer of a righteous man availeth much." Then James makes a remarkable declaration—the resulting healing will cleanse a soul both physically and spiritually: "The Lord shall raise him up; and if he have committed sins, they shall be forgiven him."

Consider the following examples of prayers of faith for the sick as recorded by Joseph Smith:

- Six p.m., I met with my Brother Hyrum, William Law, Newel K. Whitney, and Willard Richards in my private room, where we had a season of prayer for Brother Law's little daughter, who was sick, and Emma, who was somewhat better (*History of the Church* 6:31).
- Sunday . . . I arrived at the assembly room and found all present: except Hyrum and his wife. He had slipped and turned his knee joint backward, and sprained the large muscle of his leg, and I had been ministering unto him. Emma had been unwell

38

during the night. . . . We also prayed for Nathan Pratt, who was very sick, Hyrum, and others. I afterwards instructed them in the things of the Priesthood (*History of the Church* 6:98).

- A prayer-meeting held this evening in the assembly room. I was not present. Brigham Young presided. Several sick persons were prayed for (*History of the Church* 6:108).

- Prayer meeting in the evening; the brethren prayed for the sick (*History of the Church* 6:346).[94]

The Apostle Paul demonstrated the power of the prayer of faith that precedes the administration: "And it came to pass, that the father of Publius lay sick of a fever and of a bloody flux: to whom Paul entered in, *and prayed,* and laid his hands on him, and healed him."[95]

The prayer of faith and testimony.

The prayer of faith includes a *declaration of faith.* For example, upon receiving Zeezrom's request for healing, Alma and Amulek sought to increase Zeezrom's faith by urging him to focus on the Savior and declare his faith in the Lord. Note the essential steps that they followed:

> And it came to pass that Alma said unto [Zeezrom], taking him by the hand: *Believest thou in the power of Christ unto salvation?* [Alma urging him to focus on Christ and to declare his testimony.]
>
> And he answered and said: *Yea, I believe all the words that thou hast taught.* [Zeezrom's declaration of faith.]

39

And Alma said: *If thou believest in the redemption of Christ thou canst be healed.* [Again, Alma urging him to focus on Christ and to declare his faith.]

And he said: *Yea, I believe according to thy words.* [Zeezrom's declaration of faith.] And then Alma cried unto the Lord, saying: *O Lord our God, have mercy on this man, and heal him according to his faith which is in Christ.* [Alma's prayer of faith.]

And when Alma had said these words, Zeezrom leaped upon his feet, and began to walk. [The resulting physical and spiritual healing.]"[96]

In the prayer of faith, we might encourage the recipient to bear his testimony, as Alma encouraged Zeezrom. When the recipient does so, he declares his belief in and devotion to Jesus Christ. Bearing testimony is a declaration of love for the Savior: "If a man be meek and lowly in heart, and confesses by the power of the Holy Ghost that Jesus is the Christ, he must needs have charity; for if he have not charity he is nothing; wherefore he must needs have charity."[97] In return, Jesus loves and blesses the recipient with mercy and forgiveness for the testimony he has borne: "Nevertheless, ye are blessed, for the testimony which ye have borne is recorded in heaven for the angels to look upon; and they rejoice over you, and your sins are forgiven you"—an amazing blessing![98] Additionally, Jesus promises, "Whosoever shall confess me before men, him shall the Son of man also confess before the angels of God."[99] Would these promises not increase the level of faith to heal or to be healed?

Helping to increase the recipient's faith by bearing testimony.

Our bearing testimony to the recipient invokes spiritual gifts. President James E. Faust explained that spiritual gifts, such as faith to heal and faith to be healed, flow from bearing testimony and the actual administration ordinance: "The Spirit speaks peace to the soul. This spiritual solace comes by invoking [asking for] spiritual gifts, which are claimed and manifested in many ways. . . . They flow from the humble and proper use of a testimony. They also come through administering to the sick following an anointing with consecrated oil."[100] That is, by means of spiritual gifts, the Holy Ghost transmits the spiritual gift of solace or peace. When we give a priesthood blessing and it is attended by a feeling of peace, we may know by the Spirit that what has been said is true.[101] Satan cannot duplicate a feeling of peace.[102]

Testimonies borne by the elders carry healing balm into the heart of the recipient. President James E. Faust added, "Spiritual healing also comes from bearing and hearing humble testimonies. A witness given in a spirit of contrition, thankfulness for divine providence, and submission to divine guidance is a powerful remedy to help relieve the anguish and concerns of our hearts."[103] Likewise, Elder Jeffrey R. Holland, speaking to young elders, said:

> When you bear witness of [Jesus Christ] . . . you invoke the power *and the testimonies* of God the Father and the Holy

Ghost, which fulfills the law of witnesses (2 Corinthians 13:1). The Savior
Himself taught:

"Whoso believeth in me believeth
in the Father also; and unto him [the
recipient] will the Father bear record of
me, for he will visit him [the recipient]
with fire and with the Holy Ghost. And
thus will the Father bear record of me,
and the Holy Ghost will bear record
unto him [the recipient] of the Father
and me; for the Father, and I, and the
Holy Ghost are one" [3 Ne. 11:35–36].

So why should we bear frequent
and powerful testimony of Christ?
Because doing so invites and becomes
part of the divine power of testimony
borne by God the Father and by the
Holy Ghost, a testimony borne on
wings of fire to the very hearts of [recip-
ients]. Such a divine testimony of Christ
is the rock upon which every [person]
must build. Only this testimony of the
atoning Anointed, Victorious One will
prevail against the gates of hell.[104]

By bearing testimony, we elders are essentially recom-
mending Jesus to the recipient, or, in other words, bring-
ing the recipient to Christ: "And now, I would commend
you to seek this Jesus of whom the prophets and apostles
have written."[105] Moreover, by bearing testimony of Jesus
Christ and His power, both the recipient and elders can

know that God is with us: "Whosoever shall confess that Jesus is the Son of God, God dwelleth in him, and he in God."[106]

Asking

As we have learned, by divine law, *receiving* follows *asking in faith*. We, the Lord's representatives, come to the recipient in response to his request. There are two *askings* that have occurred: first, the recipient has asked the Lord for help; second, the recipient has asked us, the representatives of the Lord, to come and bless him with that for which he has asked the Lord. Unless otherwise directed by the Spirit, we elders come to grant the recipient his requested blessing, just as Jesus did. Notice in the following examples how asking in faith precedes receiving:

> And, behold, there came a leper and worshiped him, saying, Lord, if thou wilt, thou canst make me clean. And Jesus put forth his hand, and touched him, saying, I will; be thou clean. And immediately his leprosy was cleansed.[107]
>
> There came unto him a centurion, beseeching him, And saying, Lord, my servant lieth at home sick of the palsy, grievously tormented. And Jesus saith unto him, I will come and heal him.[108]
>
> Blind Bartimaeus . . . sat by the highway side begging. And when he heard that it was Jesus of Nazareth, he began to cry out, and say, Jesus, thou Son of David, have mercy on me. . . .

And Jesus answered and said unto him, What wilt thou that I should do unto thee? The blind man said unto him, Lord, that I might receive my sight. And Jesus said unto him, Go thy way; thy faith hath made thee whole. And immediately he received his sight.[109]

Regarding the elders' commission to help the recipient ask the Lord in faith for a blessing, Elder Bruce R. McConkie said, "Those called to perform the ordinance should encourage the sick person to rely on the Lord's promise. 'Whatsoever thing ye shall ask the Father in my name, which is good, in faith believing that ye shall receive, behold, it shall be done unto you.'"[110] Our emphasizing this principle to the recipient might serve to help increase his faith. President Kimball said asking in order to receive blessings has always been central to the Lord's teachings.[111] The scriptures concur:

- "If any of you lack wisdom [*or lack anything*], let him ask of God, that giveth to all men *liberally*, and upbraideth not; and it shall be given him. But let him ask in faith, nothing wavering."[112]
- "God, who has created you, on whom you are dependent for your lives and for all that ye have and are, doth grant unto you whatsoever ye ask that is right, in faith, believing that ye shall receive."[113]
- "And verily I say unto you, whatsoever things ye shall ask the Father in my name shall be given unto you. Therefore, ask, and ye shall receive; knock, and it shall be opened unto you; for he that asketh, receiveth; and unto him that knocketh, it shall be opened."[114]

- "Whatsoever thing ye shall ask in faith . . . ye shall receive it."[115]
- "Ask what ye will, and it shall be given."[116]
- "Ye are commanded in all things to ask of God."[117]

Can there be any doubt that the recipient must ask to receive? And often we must help him. Once the recipient does so in faith—taking into account the Lord's will, timing, and method—the Lord has promised that he *shall* receive. According to the LDS Bible Dictionary, we may obtain blessings from the Lord on the simple but powerful principle of *asking*. The criteria for asking are (1) acknowledging that we have a divine and eternal parent–child relationship (God is literally our Father) and (2) drawing upon that relationship to secure His blessings. Of course we must align ourselves with His will, which requires the Holy Ghost.[118] Often the blessing or healing that the recipient prayerfully asks for will be realized through a priesthood administration. Through the priesthood, we elders effectively unlock the powers of heaven so that sought-after blessings can flow to the recipient on earth.

Blessings that follow faith and asking.

In addition to the hoped-for physical healing, James describes a remarkable accompanying miracle: a recipient, as we have learned, is not only healed physically, he is healed spiritually[119]: "the Lord shall raise him up; and if he have committed sins, they shall be forgiven him."[120] "Of course [sins] will be [forgiven]," Elder Bruce R. McConkie wrote, "if [the recipient] is in tune with and receives the Spirit, for that sanctifying member of the

Godhead will not dwell in an unclean tabernacle."[121] The Lord, whose purpose is to redeem the recipient,[122] is interested in healing the person's entire soul, first spiritually and then physically. Therefore, the healing of the body is often secondary to healing the spirit. Notice the healing sequence in this episode in the Savior's ministry:

> And, behold, they brought to him a man sick of the palsy, lying on a bed: and Jesus seeing their faith said unto the sick of the palsy; Son, be of good cheer; thy sins be forgiven thee [spiritual healing].
>
> And, behold, certain of the scribes said within themselves, This man blasphemeth.
>
> And Jesus knowing their thoughts said, Wherefore think ye evil in your hearts?
>
> For whether is easier, to say, Thy sins be forgiven thee; or to say, Arise, and walk?
>
> But that ye may know that the Son of man hath power on earth to forgive sins, (then saith he to the sick of the palsy,) Arise, take up thy bed, and go unto thine house [physical healing].
>
> And he arose, and departed to his house.[123]

As we grow in our appreciation of this principle, we begin to understand why physical healing might be delayed. If our perspective were increased, we might see the Lord working on the recipient's entire soul. The Lord might heal the recipient's spirit first by working with him until he repents or modifies his thoughts and behavior. To serve that purpose, the affliction might be protracted to humble and even chastise the recipient so that his errant attitude might be burned out of him. Or the physical healing might be delayed to develop or strengthen an attribute of character to make the recipient more godlike. Elder James E. Talmage explained, "Not always are the administrations of the elders followed by immediate healings; the afflicted may be permitted to suffer in body, perhaps for the accomplishment of good purposes."[124] Elder Spencer W. Kimball expanded upon this principle:

> [The Lord] sees the end from the beginning. He knows what builds us, or tears us down, what will thwart the program and what will give us eventual triumph.
>
> [He] does not always relieve suffering and distress, for even these seemingly undesirable conditions may be part of a purposeful plan.
>
> Being human we would expel from our lives, sorrow, distress, physical pain and mental anguish and assure ourselves of continual ease and comfort, but if we closed the doors upon such [difficulties], we might be evicting our greatest friends and benefactors. Suffering can make saints of people as they learn patience, long suffering and self-mastery.

The sufferings of our Savior [were] part of his education. . . .

I'm positive in my mind that the Lord has planned our destiny. We shorten our lives but I think we cannot lengthen them very much. Sometime we'll understand fully, and when we see back from the vantage point of the future we shall be satisfied with many of the happenings of this life which seemed so difficult for us to comprehend.[125]

Of course, the causes for delayed healing and the process are not ours to judge. Specific priesthood keys are required for such judgments. Our responsibility is to faithfully administer the administration ordinance by the inspiration of the Spirit, then leave the details of the blessing to be worked out between the recipient and the Lord.

CHAPTER 6
A LIFE RESCUED AND
RECONSECRATED TO THE LORD

Because an associated blessing of the administration ordinance is spiritual healing,[126] the recipient's asking might include rededicating himself to God. This is not to suggest that the recipient should bargain for deliverance, which would be improper, i.e., *If you heal me then I will do such and such.* Rather, rededicating one's life to God is realigning and recommitting one's self to one's covenants. Elder John A. Widtsoe said:

> Ordinances give life to faith because they require a covenant from those who participate. Faith is a principle that demands action. Whether it is faith in a law, doctrine, or plan relative to human affairs, it fails unless it leads to a practice, rite, or ceremony. Otherwise it remains an idle belief, an abstract conviction, a theory. The moment it is used, as in an ordinance, it flames into life, and leaps into the world of practical affairs, becoming a positive power, helpful in the world of men. . . .

49

Everyone who receives an ordinance must make a covenant, else the ordinance is not fully satisfactory . . . [both] he who is administered to for sickness and the administrators, covenant to use their faith to secure the desired healings.[127]

Healing Is Symbolic of Christ's Power to Deliver

Being rescued from sickness and affliction by the power of the priesthood might be viewed as symbolic of Christ's power to deliver us from all our enemies,[128] including spiritual and physical death. Quoting President Harold B. Lee, gospel writers Joseph Fielding McConkie and Robert L. Millet wrote:

> It may be that all of the miraculous healings performed by Jesus were but tangible symbols of the greatest healing that he alone could perform—the healing of sick spirits and the cleansing of sin-stained souls. "The greatest miracles I see today," declared President Harold B. Lee, "are not necessarily the healing of sick bodies, but the . . . healing of sick souls, those who are sick in soul and spirit and are downhearted and distraught, on the verge of nervous breakdowns" (*Conference Report,* April 1973, 178).[129]

A sickness or affliction reminds a person of his fallen state, which drives him to recognize his helplessness without the Lord's intervention.[130] That is, because of the Fall, the person is suffering in this weakened situation, but he knows that Jesus Christ has overcome the Fall. With that hope, the afflicted person humbly beseeches the Lord for help, then calls for the Lord's authorized priesthood representatives—whom the afflicted person recognizes as those having the power of Jesus Christ—to answer the person's request. The elders come in response.

In a sincere prayer of faith (by the afflicted person, a friend, loved one, or the elders), the person humbly declares his testimony of the Lord, his belief that the Lord can heal him through His servants from these specific effects of the Fall, and asks the Lord for healing.[131]

The elders then perform the ordinance of administration by the laying on of hands and by means of the power of the name of Jesus Christ.[132] Because the administration is *sealed*, it is recognized in heaven and on earth,[133] and the Lord promises to confirm or validate it.[134]

Through the administration ordinance, powers on earth and in heaven are set in motion, and the Lord now begins the process of healing the person both spiritually and physically. When the healing process is completed, the Fall has symbolically been overcome, and the once-afflicted person is in a position to bear heightened testimony of the reality of the Savior, His power to deliver, and the certainty of the restoration of the gospel and priesthood.

Afflictions Consecrated to God "for the Welfare of Thy Soul"

Elder Gerald N. Lund taught that the consecrated oil suggests consecrating or reconsecrating a life: "Consecrated olive oil is always used to consecrate or reconsecrate a life—to sanctify [it]."[135] In the context of consecration as it applies to administering to the sick, Elder Bruce R. McConkie wrote, "How aptly Nephi said: . . . 'Ye must not perform any thing unto the Lord save in the first place ye shall pray unto the Father in the name of Christ, that he will consecrate thy performance unto thee, that thy performance may be for the welfare of thy soul' [2 Ne. 32:9]."[136]

When a covenant person petitions the Lord for a blessing, that person's affliction is in effect *consecrated to him* "for the welfare of [his] soul." That is, "all things [even sickness and afflictions] shall work together for [his] good."[137] We can even place our sicknesses and afflictions upon the altar of faith and the Lord will count them as consecrated offerings that will sanctify us and bring us closer to God.

In the process of receiving a blessing, the person has the opportunity to rededicate or reconsecrate his life to the Lord, who has rescued him spiritually and physically. *Consecrate* means "dedicated to a sacred purpose,"[138] or in other words to be set apart as holy, to be completely devoted to the Lord. The person is thereby reconsecrated to a sacred purpose, set apart as holy, and completely devoted to the Lord, who has saved him.

CHAPTER 7
THE ADMINISTRATION ORDINANCE

Since the procedure for administering to the sick and afflicted is stated in the *Church Handbook of Instructions* (Book 2, pages 172–73), in this chapter we will only discuss the ordinance generally and examine its parts.

Elder Bruce R. McConkie wrote, "Administrations are of two parts: anointings and sealings; both performances are accompanied by the laying on of hands."[139] He also stated that the anointing is performed with "pure olive oil" that has been set apart for the holy purpose of anointing the sick.[140] The anointing is done by one elder, and normally two or more elders seal the anointing.[141]

Because two or more elders perform this ordinance, we might imagine the fulfillment of the Law of Witnesses: "In the mouth of two or three witnesses shall every word be established."[142] Also, because this ordinance calls for two or more elders, we might recognize another significant principle that could serve to increase our faith: "Verily, verily, I say unto you, as I said unto my disciples, where two or three are gathered together in my name, as touching one thing, behold, there will I be in the midst of them—even so am I in the midst of you."[143]

Laying on of Hands

The Lord has provided a symbol that suggests a tangible bridge or conduit over or through which blessings are, according to Elder McConkie, "convey[ed]" from God through His authorized servants to recipients. That is to say, "they must feel the hands of the Lord's servants on their heads as the words . . . are spoken."[144] *True to the Faith* explains laying on of hands this way:

> The laying on of hands is the procedure revealed by the Lord for performing many priesthood ordinances, such as confirmation, ordination, setting members apart to serve in callings, administering to the sick, and giving other priesthood blessings [see D&C 42:44; A of F 1:4–5]. Those having the proper priesthood authority place their hands upon the head of the person receiving the ordinance. In doing so, they serve as instruments through whom the Lord blesses His children [see D&C 36:2].[145]

Anointing with Consecrated Olive Oil

The anointing is the first part of the administration ordinance.[146] To administer means "to give or apply in a formal way" or "to apply as a remedy."[147] To anoint means "to apply oil . . . during a religious ceremony as a sign of sanctification or consecration."[148] Therefore, the anointing suggests that the elders are administering a sacred remedy to the afflicted person by means of a formal ordinance. Viewed another way, the elders are performing the anointing with the faith that it will sanctify or consecrate the afflicted person so that the remedy can become effective. In any case, the anointing is highly charged with rich symbolism.

President Spencer W. Kimball added another purpose for the anointing: "[When] an elder pours a small quantity of oil on the head of the one to be blessed . . . by authority of the priesthood, *he anoints the person for the restoration of health.*" [149]

The symbolism of olive oil.

Only pure, consecrated olive oil is used for the administration ordinance. (Again, the procedure for consecrating oil is stated in the *Church Handbook of Instructions, Book 2*, pages 172–73.) It is interesting to note that olive oil burns without giving off smoke, which lends to its symbolism of purity.

"The reason for using olive oil rather than any other kind of oil is never clearly stated in the scriptures. . . . The olive branch has long been a token of peace. The olive tree is used in scripture as a symbol for the house of Israel [Hosea 14:6; Rom. 11:17; Jacob 5; D&C 101:43–62]." [150] As to the symbolism of olive oil, Elder Theodore M. Burton said, "Oil is the sacred symbol of the spirit's operations." [151] Echoing that idea, Elder Gerald N. Lund wrote:

> It is important to remember that physical symbols are used to represent spiritual things. The olive tree represents peace and purity (*Doctrines of Salvation*

3:180). In the introduction to D&C 88, Joseph Smith suggests that the Tree of Paradise (Tree of Life) was an olive tree. The ancient Menorah or sacred candlestick in the Tabernacle and later in the temple was a representation of the Tree of Life. Its seven cups held olive oil that burned continually, representing the fire of the Holy Ghost. *Thus olive oil is a symbol of the Holy Ghost and its [the Spirit's] power to provide peace and to purify.*[152]

On another occasion, Elder Lund taught the following:

"The olive tree from the earliest times has been the emblem of peace and purity" [*Doctrines of Salvation,* 3:180]. Also, in the Parable of the Ten Virgins, the wise were prepared with oil [see Matt. 25:1–13]. Modern revelation equates that preparation (having olive oil) with taking "the Holy Spirit for their guide" [D&C 45:55–57]. To touch with oil suggests the effect of the Spirit on the same organs of living and acting that had previously been cleansed by the blood of Christ. Thus, every aspect of the candidate's life was purified and sanctified by both the Atonement and the Holy Ghost.[153]

Olive oil has other symbolisms. For example, the *Encyclopedia of Mormonism* states:

> Two New Testament parables illustrate possible symbolisms of oil both as a therapeutic ointment and as a source of light. The good Samaritan, finding the injured traveler, "bound up his wounds, pouring in oil and wine" (Luke 10:34). In another parable, wise virgins "took oil in their vessels with their lamps" and thus were in possession of material to provide light, to celebrate the coming of the bridegroom, Christ (Matt. 25:1–13).[154]

Elder Jeffrey R. Holland also commented on the significance of olive oil, beginning his thoughts with a quote from Truman Madsen:

> "One Jewish legend identifies the tree of life as the olive tree, and with good reason. The olive tree is an evergreen, not a deciduous tree. Its leaves do not seasonally fade nor fall. Through scorching heat and winter cold they are continually rejuvenated." As Lehi himself taught, no symbol could serve more powerfully and profoundly of God's expansive, constant, redeeming love—including especially the love represented in the gift of his Only Begotten Son—than does

the olive tree. . . . The oil from the olive vineyards was everywhere present in ancient Israel, even as it is today. It is a staple in every kitchen for cooking and on every table for seasoning. It serves medicinally as an antidote for poison and an ointment for pain. It is burned for light in the smallest of lamps and for fuel in the largest of homes. In more sacred purposes it is used in anointing the sick, in purification and sacrifice, and in the consecration of priests and kings. As it was for Noah, so today is the olive branch a symbol of peace—with its obvious typological source in the Prince of Peace. . . . Olive oil is still used in the careful preparation of the paschal lamb at the Feast of the Passover.

Christ ascended from and will return to his beloved Mount of Olives. Gethsemane is literally the "garden of the oil press." Christ is ultimately the Anointed One. Surely the majesty of Christ is inextricably linked with the olive grove, and no teaching explores that symbolism more profoundly than the Book of Mormon.[155]

The anointing, therefore, should bring to mind the healing, sanctifying, purifying effect of the Holy Ghost, whose earthly symbol is olive oil. By anointing a suffering person with olive oil "for the restoration of health,"[156] we are in effect anointing him with the Holy Ghost (or the blood of Jesus Christ through the Holy Ghost) to save and "reconsecrate his life"[157] both physically and spiritually. An endowment of the Spirit always brings light, understanding, power, and healing. Through the healing process, a recipient may be rescued and redeemed by the power of the Atonement of Jesus Christ.

Sealing the Anointing

Because *sealing* is so closely associated with the temple, sealing the anointing should be regarded with profound reverence.

On April 3, 1836, in the Kirtland Temple, Elijah restored the keys of the sealing power to Joseph Smith and Oliver Cowdery.[158] To seal is "to perform certain acts on earth and have them recognized (sealed) or validated in heaven."[159] To Peter, the Lord said, "And I will give unto thee the keys of the kingdom of heaven: and whatsoever thou shalt bind on earth shall be bound in heaven: and whatsoever thou shalt loose on earth shall be loosed in heaven."[160]

The president of the Church holds all the keys of the sealing power, which keys flow down to priesthood leaders and priesthood holders so they can perform their duties—such as baptisms and other ordinances of salvation and comfort. "What might be called the general sealing power is . . . vested in the President of the Church," wrote Elder McConkie. *"Everyone who receives the priesthood obtains this general sealing power to a degree. . . .* All things gain enduring force and validity because of the sealing power."[161] Although administering to the sick is not a saving ordinance, it is nevertheless sealed and therefore recognized as valid in heaven.

Priesthood Blessing as the Spirit Inspires

Typically, an inspired blessing follows the anointing and sealing. The blessing might be viewed as given in response to what was requested in the prayer of faith. As the Spirit directs, the blessing opens the door to an endowment of healing power and/or comfort.

Often, priesthood holders rush into an administration without spending time talking to the recipient to determine his level of faith and to gain his trust. If, as has been stated, we find that his faith is lacking, we might try to help him increase it. This process often requires time as we work with the recipient and listen carefully to the Spirit. Again, Jesus set the example of talking with people and asking them questions to ascertain, then help them with, their faith. Sometimes he took them aside, possibly so they could better focus on Him and not be distracted. Consider the following incident:

> And he cometh to Bethsaida; and they bring a blind man unto him, and besought him to touch him [administer to him].
>
> And he took the blind man by the hand, and led him out of the town [perhaps so the man could focus on Christ without distraction]; and when [Jesus] had spit on his eyes [it's possible that touching the blind man helped to increase his faith], and put his hands upon [the man], he asked him if he saw ought [Jesus took the time to be with and talk to the man].

And [the man] looked up, and said, I see men as trees, walking.

After that [Jesus] put his hands again upon his eyes, and made him look up: and he was restored, and saw every man clearly [Jesus kept working with the man until the healing was complete].[162]

When we feel that the recipient is ready and when we feel that we have the Lord's permission, we bless the person and, as President Kimball stated, "pronounce such blessings as seem appropriate and as the Spirit moves."[163]

After the Savior had spent time talking with the Nephites, he perceived that their faith was sufficient to be healed. Only then did he proceed: "Have ye any that are sick among you? Bring them hither. . . . I perceive that ye desire that I should show unto you what I have done unto your brethren at Jerusalem, *for I see that your faith is sufficient that I should heal you.*"[164]

Finally, when we have ascertained and lifted a recipient's faith, and when we pronounce the blessing, we do not *address the Lord or ask Him to heal.* Asking is what we do in the prayer of faith. When we perform the administration, we *address the recipient* and *bless, invoke, rebuke* and/or *command* by the power of the priesthood and in the name of Jesus Christ.

Other Provisions

As the *Church Handbook of Instructions* (Book 2, pages 172–73) lists provisions and instructions for giving blessings, including provisions for multiple priesthood holders participating in the administration, and when not to obtain a priesthood leader's permission, those topics are not covered in this book.

CHAPTER 8
POWER IN THE ATONEMENT

Because of Christ's perfect knowledge, He foresaw then suffered for every one of our afflictions. And the Savior overcame them! He overcame them *in advance.* In the Atonement, Jesus gained, in effect, the *keys of deliverance* for each specific affliction. Believing in Christ's individualized foreknowledge of us, and His suffering for and victory over all our *enemies* is essential to our faith in Him.

> And he shall go forth, suffering pains and afflictions and temptations of every kind; and this that the word might be fulfilled which saith he will take upon him the pains and the sicknesses of his people.
>
> And he will take upon him death, that he may loose the bands of death which bind his people; and he will take upon him their infirmities, that his bowels may be filled with mercy, according to the flesh, that he may know according to the flesh how to succor his people according to their infirmities.[165]

As representatives of Jesus Christ, we call upon the Lord and seek the deliverance *that He has already accomplished.* When we consider the terrible price that Jesus paid to overcome this present affliction, we would be remiss if we imagined that He would not be anxious to help. Jesus Christ is called Savior, Redeemer, Deliverer, and the Great Physician for a reason, and that reason is to save, redeem, deliver, and heal. Our faith hinges on our belief that He is all these things and more. "Every aspect of a person's life is touched and affected by the atonement of Christ."[166]

Because the Atonement is constantly effective in our lives, the recipient can believe with full confidence that his specific affliction was contemplated, suffered for, and overcome by the Savior. Therefore, a solution is *at hand* if the recipient has the faith to take the Savior *by the hand,* believe in Him, hearken to His counsel, and by seeking inspiration follow the same course that the Savior followed to overcome the affliction. "Come follow me," He said.[167] The priesthood opens the door to the Lord's solution in the Atonement.

And a solution will come.

Jesus Christ is the Great Physician with "healing in his wings,"[168] who "healeth the broken in heart, and bindeth up their wounds."[169] And He does this through "the Comforter . . . the agent of healing,"[170] President James E. Faust writes:

> We find solace in Christ *through the agency of the Comforter,* and the Savior extends this invitation to us: "Come unto me, all ye that labour and are

heavy laden, and I will give you rest" [Matt. 11:28]. The Apostle Peter speaks of "casting all your care upon him; for he careth for you" [1 Pet. 5:7]. As we do this, healing takes place, just as the Lord promised through the prophet Jeremiah when He said: "I will turn their mourning into joy, and will comfort them, and make them rejoice from their sorrow. . . . I have satiated the weary soul, and I have replenished every sorrowful soul" [Jer. 31:13, 25].

And in the celestial glory, we are told that "God shall wipe away all tears from their eyes; and there shall be no more death, neither sorrow, nor crying, neither shall there be any more pain" [Rev. 21:4]. Then faith and hope will replace heartache, disappointment, torment, anguish, and despair, and the Lord will give us strength, as Mormon says, that we "should suffer no manner of afflictions, save it were swallowed up in the joy of Christ" [Alma 31:38].[171]

The Principle of Grace as It Applies to Healing

Nowhere in the process of administering to the sick and afflicted can we escape the necessity of faith in the Lord Jesus Christ. Only by means of His power and grace can elders heal and recipients be healed. According to the LDS Bible Dictionary, *grace* is a divine means of help or strength, and it originates with and is only available through Jesus Christ. Grace is an outgrowth of His mercy and love. Grace provides us strength to be more than we are and do more than we could do on our own.[172] When we recognize our weakness, inability, and that we truly are nothing without him,[173] we are driven to Christ to plead for His grace.

To demonstrate the divine strength that is available through the Lord's grace, Elder David A. Bednar recited the incident when Nephi's brothers bound him: "It is especially interesting to me that Nephi did not pray . . . to have his circumstances changed. Rather, *he prayed for the strength to change his circumstances*," thus drawing on "the enabling power of the atonement of the Savior."[174] Strength to change the circumstance comes by drawing upon the Lord's power, which is often transmitted by means of priesthood administrations.

Whenever we bring our needs to the Lord, we are obligated to do all we can to qualify for His help, "for we know that it is by grace that we are saved, after all we can do."[175] Therefore, elders should encourage the recipient to do all that is within his power, then leave everything else to the Lord. President Brigham Young said, "It appears consistent to me to apply every remedy that comes within the range of my knowledge, and to ask my Father in Heaven, in the name of Jesus Christ, to sanctify that application to the healing of my body."[176]

An interesting phenomenon that often accompanies an administration is the recipient's becoming more sick and needing medical care. Without an understanding of the priesthood and the Lord's grace, this can create questions and diminish faith. But the mature priesthood holder understands that the principle of grace requires all that we can do with the assurance that the Lord will make up the difference. The priesthood is the directing power, and the administration sets in motion a series of events that lead to healing, in whatever form the Lord wishes the healing to take place. Because the Lord makes the effort to reveal medical knowledge, he expects us to research and take advantage of His revelation. If there is a gap between revealed medical knowledge and what is necessary for healing, grace steps in and makes up the difference. In any case, utilizing the priesthood to draw down directing power is the proper course of action. Clearly we want the Lord involved in the healing process. Then we must do all we can with the resources He has provided, and with faith that grace will make up the difference, and then we watch for the miracle to occur.

Of course, sometimes "all that we can do" is very little or nothing. Nevertheless, a little goes a long way. The widow's mite was sufficient to summon the Lord's favor,[177] and in the case of the snake-bitten Israelites, all that the Lord required was that they look upon the brass serpent to be healed.[178] We must remember that healings are as unique as the individuals who receive them; and we must also remember that a healing is an unearned gift given by Jesus Christ as an outgrowth of His compassion and His grace.

CHAPTER 9
WHEN THE ANSWER IS NO
OR NOT NOW

President Harold B. Lee taught that all of our prayers are answered, but sometimes the Lord says *no*.[179]

A *no* or *not now* answer tests the faith of everyone—the recipient, the elders, and those who are praying or caring for the recipient. When a healing is not forthcoming, we might benefit by remembering past manifestations of God's love and former evidences of His reality that speak to His concern for and relationship with us. We might ask ourselves, "Does God really exist? If so, does He know me, care about me, and love me? Does He have the power or interest to heal me?" Or perhaps we chastise ourselves by rehearsing past mistakes: "I can't heal or be healed because I am not worthy enough." Or maybe we despair that we do not have enough faith to be healed.

But in all this despairing, we are remiss.

We are not dealing with an imagined, unknown, fickle, uncaring, judgmental, graceless God. The true God whom we worship is a perfectly consistent, loving, knowledgeable, powerful, compassionate God, who does not favor one person over another, who is incapable of lying, and who is full of grace to enable our weak faith.

Once we admit these truths, we rally around the myriad promises that He has made concerning faith, deliverance, grace, asking and receiving, and healing. Then, filled with testimony, we, like the father of the lunatic child, cry out with tears in our eyes, "Lord, I believe; help thou mine unbelief."[180] We cry out with Job, "Though he slay me, yet will I trust in him" and "till I die I will not remove mine integrity from me."[181] We cry out with Alma, "I have been supported under trials and troubles of every kind, yea, and in all manner of afflictions; yea, God has delivered me from prison, and from bonds, and from death; yea, *and I do put my trust in him, and he will still deliver me.*"[182]

When the healing does not arrive or when it comes in tiny steps that require protracted endurance, we can draw comfort from the account of the Savior in Gethsemane: "And he was withdrawn from them about a stone's cast, and kneeled down, and prayed, Saying, Father, if thou be willing, remove this cup from me: nevertheless not my will, but thine, be done. *And there appeared an angel unto him from heaven, strengthening him.*"[183]

Though God may say *no* or *not now* and allow us, as Elder James E. Talmage said, "to suffer in body, perhaps for the accomplishment of good purposes,"[184] He will never leave us without comfort. We can fully expect to receive heavenly help, as did Jesus, to give us the strength to press forward with faith.

The Gift of Peace
Often the process of being healed or enduring when the answer is *no* or *not now* is accompanied by a feeling of

peace in the midst of the turbulence. When Joseph Smith cried, "O God, where art thou?" the Lord responded, "My son, peace be unto thy soul."[185] As we have discussed, peace is an unduplicatable spiritual gift that can only come from the Lord through the Holy Ghost.[186] The feeling of peace, which indicates the companionship of the Comforter, provides us with an increased capacity to endure even when the odds seem staggering or when we sweat our own great drops of blood in the Gethsemanes of our lives.

The Lord's Timing

The Lord said, "My words are sure and shall not fail. . . . But all things must come to pass in their time."[187] Faith and trust are synonymous terms. If we claim to have faith in Jesus Christ, we are also claiming that we trust him. When we say, "Thy will be done," we are saying, "We trust thy way of doing things and thy timetable." We back off on attempting to impose our questionable and possibly imperfect timetable upon God, who is perfect. We have the Lord's word that he will keep his promises: "[He] will hasten [his] work in its time."[188]

Elder Neal A. Maxwell said, "Our faith in God includes faith in God's timing, enough to be able to say, in effect, 'Thy timing be done.' . . . When we are impatient, in effect, we do not honor what is implied in the words 'in process of time.' We foolishly wish to have some of life's moments over and done with, seasons to be over with, ignoring the possibilities for service that are inherent in them."[189] If we can truly believe He has our welfare at heart, may we not let His plans unfold as He thinks best? God will bless us "in his own time, and in his own way, and according to his own will."[190]

Because we know that "he is a God of truth and cannot lie,"[191] we can persist in faith despite life's obstacles and circumstances beyond our control, believing that deliverance, according to His definition and timing, will come. When the timing is long and uncertain, we can take comfort in the words of the Savior to the early Saints who suffered so much:

> Verily I say unto you my friends, fear not, let your hearts be comforted; yea, rejoice evermore, and in everything give thanks;
>
> Waiting patiently on the Lord, for your prayers have entered into the ears of the Lord of Sabaoth, and are recorded with this seal and testament—*the Lord hath sworn and decreed that they shall be granted.*
>
> *Therefore, he giveth this promise unto you, with an immutable covenant that they shall be fulfilled; and all things wherewith you have been afflicted shall work together for your good,* and to my name's glory, saith the Lord.[192]

The Cry of Allegiance in the Midst of Trial

An affliction consecrated "to [His] name's glory" is one that produces an ancillary miracle in the healing process—an increase in testimony that allows us to bear witness of the Lord's divinity. Such a borne testimony is a cry of allegiance in the midst of affliction. It strengthens the faith of both believers and unbelievers. Apparently, some people are allowed to suffer so that the Lord might work a miracle in their lives to draw attention to the Savior's reality and the power of the restored gospel and priesthood.

The story of the Lord's raising Lazarus is such an example: "Now a certain man was sick, named Lazarus, of Bethany, the town of Mary and her sister Martha. . . .Therefore his sisters sent unto him, saying, Lord, behold, he whom thou lovest is sick. When Jesus heard that, he said, *This sickness is not unto death, but for the glory of God, that the Son of God might be glorified thereby.*"[193] The next verse is perhaps one of the most important in the story. "Now Jesus loved Martha, and her sister, and Lazarus."[194] It seems that John wanted to make it perfectly clear that the affliction had nothing to do with Lazarus, Mary, or Martha's unworthiness or Jesus' being unfeeling toward them. The affliction had everything to do with trust and love.

Imagine! The Lord trusted His beloved friends to endure a terrible trial, which they did not understand at the time, all for the purpose of glorifying Him—to demonstrate who He was and His power of redemption. Therefore, to this end, Jesus delayed His coming. During that time Lazarus died and was buried.

When the Lord finally arrived, Lazarus had lain in the grave four days. Mary and Martha were grief-stricken but not disillusioned. With unwavering faith, they individually bore their testimonies of the Master. It seems that possibly this scene of fierce discipleship (not the scene of Lazarus's death, for within minutes Lazarus would come forth) overwhelmed Jesus, and He wept.

The Savior trusted these friends to be the instruments through which He could be glorified, so that other people might believe and be healed. Their demonstration of loyalty in the midst of apparent tragedy proved them worthy, and now they would be rewarded. He asked, "Where have ye laid him?"[195] They took him to the grave and rolled away the stone. Jesus reminded Martha, "Said I not unto thee, that, if thou wouldest believe, thou shouldest *see the glory of God?*"[196] The reference indicates the power of God to heal or reverse the impossible. Imagine how that tiny seed of hope must have swelled within Martha and Mary. Jesus offered a prayer of gratitude to His Father, and then He "cried with a loud voice, Lazarus, come forth. And he that was dead came forth, bound hand and foot with graveclothes: and his face was bound about with a napkin. Jesus saith unto them, Loose him, and let him go. Then many of the Jews which came to Mary, and had seen the things which Jesus did, believed on him."[197]

The trial was over and the Son of God was glorified. And here is an essential point of the story that all of us should try to understand: Many unbelievers who witnessed the miracle became believers, and the believers were strengthened in their faith. How? *By the Lord's showing forth His power to heal a devastating affliction when apparently the situation was beyond hope.* The Savior had relied on His beloved friends to suffer without perspective so that He could effect a miraculous healing, demonstrate the glorifying power of God, and draw souls unto Him. Do we have enough faith to allow the Savior to use us in a like manner?

Nurturing the Sick and Afflicted

When the answer is *no* or *not now,* we commend the sick or afflicted into the hands of those who will nourish them "with all tenderness, with herbs and mild food."[198] President Joseph F. Smith stated, "But the healing of a wound is an art not acquired by practice alone, but by the loving tenderness that comes from universal good will and a sympathetic interest in the welfare and happiness of others."[199] This is an act of faith, not resignation. By following the Lord's counsel, we are holding fast to the *words of God* that have been spoken by the Lord's representatives and with the hope that with patience we will yet prevail. "For I know that thou wast in bonds; yea, and I also know that thou wast stoned for the word's sake; and thou didst bear all these things with patience because the Lord was with thee; *and now thou knowest that the Lord did deliver thee.*"[200]

Patience is not so much *enduring* as it is *waiting with hope, expectation, and assurance.* Patience is an essential quality of God's *charity.* Patience means: "I will wait *with* you" or "I will wait *for* you" or "I will wait *upon* you," but one way or another *I will wait.* Patience is a divine virtue that we all count on—we expect God to be patient. Since we are in the process of becoming like God, we should not be surprised that He gives us opportunities to develop this supernal attribute. Someone has said, "There could be nothing as frightening as an impatient God." Charity *waits.*

CHAPTER 10
WE ARE SET APART FOR A
LIFE OF SERVICE

Our commission in the priesthood can be found in Jesus' instructions to His Apostles: "And as ye go, preach, saying, The kingdom of heaven is at hand [i.e. we come in the name of Jesus Christ with His authority, which are evidences of the kingdom of heaven]. Heal the sick, cleanse the lepers, raise the dead, cast out devils: *freely ye have received, freely give.*"[201]

Later, after Jesus' Resurrection and ascension, Peter and John approached the temple and came in contact with a lame man who was daily laid at the gate of the temple in order to beg. Seeing Peter and John about to go into the temple [he] asked an alms:

> And Peter, fastening his eyes upon him with John, said, Look on us.
>
> And he gave heed unto them, expecting to receive something of them.
>
> Then Peter said, Silver and gold have I none; *but such as I have give I thee:* In the name of Jesus Christ of Nazareth rise up and walk.

> And he took him by the right hand, and lifted him up: and immediately his feet and ankle bones received strength.
>
> And he leaping up stood, and walked, and entered with them into the temple, walking, and leaping, and praising God.[202]

The "such" that Peter and John had was the priesthood of God, which they had received freely, and the blessings of which they then gave freely. This should be our model. Speaking of giving freely what we have received, President Brigham Young said,

> A man who wishes to receive light and knowledge, to increase in the faith of the Holy Gospel, and to grow in the knowledge of the truth as it is in Jesus Christ, will find that when he imparts knowledge to others he will also grow and increase. Be not miserly in your feelings, but get knowledge and understanding by freely imparting it to others, and be not like a man who selfishly hoards his gold; for that man will not thus increase upon the amount, but will become contracted in his views and feelings. So the man who will not impart freely of the knowledge he has received, will become so contracted in his mind that he cannot receive truth when it is presented to him. *Wherever you see an*

opportunity to do good, do it, for that is the way to increase and grow in the knowledge of the truth.[203]

An Apostolic Prayer

Listing the elements of effectual physical and spiritual healing, Elder Bruce R. McConkie offered this fervent prayer in General Conference:

> O Father . . . there are those among us who are sick and afflicted, who suffer from disease, and who are not appointed unto death. O thou Great Physician, pour out thy healing power upon thy Saints.
>
> O Lord, increase our faith, and let the sick be healed and the dead raised even in greater numbers than at present.
>
> But above this, O thou God of healing, wilt thou cause him who came with healing in his wings also to heal us spiritually.[204]

May this be our prayer and the prayer of those to whom we freely administer.

ENDNOTES

1. James 5:14.
2. Matthew 10:8.
3. Matthew Cowley, *BYU Speeches of the Year:* April 5, 1966.
4. Hyrum L. Andrus and Helen Mae Andrus, comps., *They Knew the Prophet,* 61.
5. Bruce R. McConkie, "Administrations," *Mormon Doctrine,* 22.
6. Matthew 4:23–24.
7. Hyrum L. Andrus and Helen Mae Andrus, *They Knew the Prophet*, 82–83.
8. See Bruce R. McConkie, "Administrations," *Mormon Doctrine,* 21–23, original emphasis removed.
9. See "Ordinances and Blessings," *Church Handbook of Instructions,* 173.
10. Bruce R. McConkie, "Ordinances," *Mormon Doctrine,* 548.
11. See "Ordinances," *Encyclopedia of Mormonism,"* 1032.
12. "Ordinances," *Encyclopedia of Mormonism,* 1032–33, original styles removed.

13. "Ordinances," *Encyclopedia of Mormonism,* 1032–33, original styles removed.
14. 2 Corinthians 12:7.
15. See James E. Talmage, *Articles of Faith,* 205.
16. D&C 42:44, 48, emphasis added.
17. Spencer W. Kimball, *Tragedy or Destiny,* a devotional assembly at Brigham Young University, December 6, 1955.
18. D&C 42:43.
19. Bruce R. McConkie, *A New Witness for the Articles of Faith,* 379.
20. See Isaiah 55:8.
21. D&C 42:48–51, emphasis added.
22. Luke 22:42.
23. See D&C 107:3.
24. Alma 13:3.
25. Romans 8:29.
26. Alma 13:3.
27. Alma 13:2.
28. J. Reuben Clark, Jr., *Conference Report,* October 1950, 170–71, emphasis added; See Abraham 3:22–23.
29. See Joseph Smith, *Lectures on Faith* 3:2–5.
30. See Joseph Smith, *Lectures on Faith* 3:12–18.
31. See Joseph Smith, *Lectures on Faith* 4.
32. See D&C 121:36–46; See also H. Burke Petersen, "Priesthood—Authority and Power," *Ensign,* May 1976, 32–34.
33. Moroni 10:4.
34. Mosiah 3:19.
35. See Bruce R. McConkie, *A New Witness for the Articles of Faith,* 176–177.
36. Jacob 4:9, emphasis added.

37. D&C 1:38, emphasis added.

38. See D&C 128:8.

39. D&C 1:38.

40. Joseph Smith, *Lectures on Faith* 7:3, emphasis added.

41. Moses 7:13, emphasis added.

42. Hebrews 11:3, emphasis added.

43. Mormon 9:17, emphasis added.

44. 1 Nephi 17:26, emphasis added.

45. Moses 1:29–30, 32, emphasis added.

46. See John 1 chapter heading and 1:1.

47. D&C 84:19–21, emphasis added.

48. Abraham 1:18, emphasis added.

49. Luke 10:9, comments added.

50. Luke 10:17, emphasis added.

51. See Ephesians 1:5; 2:19.

52. D&C 18:21–24, emphasis and comments added.

53. JST Genesis 14:30–31.

54. Mormon 9:24, emphasis and comments added.

55. Mormon 9:24, see D&C 132:59, comments added.

56. "Healing the Sick," *Discourses of Brigham Young*, 162.

57. See Exodus 20:7.

58. D&C 63:61–62, 63.

59. *History of The Church of Jesus Christ of Latter-day Saints,* 4:4–5.

60. *History of The Church of Jesus Christ of Latter-day Saints,* 4:7.

61. Jacob 4:6, emphasis added.

62. Jacob 4:7, emphasis added.

63. D&C 46:20.

64. See "Fasting and Prayer," *Duties and Blessings of the Priesthood: Basic Manual for Priesthood Holders, Part A, Lesson 31.*

65. Isaiah 58:6, 9, 12, comments added.

66. Luke 10:9.

67. Matthew Cowley, *BYU Speeches of the Year:* April 5, 1966, comments added.

68. Bruce R. McConkie, *A New Witness for the Articles of Faith,* 379.

69. See D&C 84:33–40.

70. D&C 66:9; see Mark 16:18.

71. D&C 36:2, emphasis added.

72. D&C 35:14.

73. D&C 1:38, emphasis added.

74. Joseph Fielding Smith, "Our Responsibility As Priesthood Holders," *Ensign,* June 1971, 49.

75. Howard W. Hunter, "Reading the Scriptures," *Ensign,* November 1979, 64–65.

76. D&C 4:7.

77. D&C 121:36.

78. See "Faith," LDS Bible Dictionary.

79. John 16:24, emphasis added.

80. D&C 46:7.

81. D&C 46:8, comments added.

82. D&C 35:8–9, emphasis added.

83. 1 John 5:14–15.

84. 1 Nephi 1:14.

85. Mark 2:1–11.

86. Mark 5:22–43.

87. See Matthew 8:5–13.

88. D&C 24:13–14, emphasis and comments added; see James 5:14.

89. Mark 9:23–24.

90. Matthew 9:27–30.

91. Spencer W. Kimball, "President Kimball Speaks Out on Administration to the Sick," *New Era,* October 1981.

92. Spencer W. Kimball, "President Kimball Speaks Out on Administration to the Sick," *New Era,* October 1981, emphasis added.

93. James 5:14–16, emphasis added.

94. List compiled by Rulon T.Burton, *We Believe,* 661–62.

95. Acts 28:8, emphasis added.

96. Alma 15:6–11, emphasis and comments added.

97. Moroni 7:44.

98. D&C 62:3.

99. Luke 12:8.

100. James E. Faust, "He Healeth the Broken in Heart," *Ensign*, July 2005, comments added.

101. See "I Have a Question," *Ensign* October 1993; See S. Dilworth Young, "The Still Small Voice," *Ensign*, May 1976.

102. See George Q. Cannon, *Journal of Discourses* 15, 379.

103. James E. Faust, "He Healeth the Broken in Heart," *Ensign,* July 2005.

104. Jeffrey R. Holland, "Missionary Work and the Atonement," *Liahona,* October 2001.

105. Ether 12:41.

106. 1 John 4:15.

107. Matthew 8:2–3.

108. Matthew 8:5–7.

109. Mark 10:46–47, 51–52.

110. Bruce R. McConkie, *Mormon Doctrine,* 22, quoting Moroni 7:26.

111. See Spencer W. Kimball, "President Kimball Speaks Out on Administration to the Sick," *New Era,* October 1981.

112. James 1:5–6, emphasis and comments added.

113. Mosiah 4:21.

114. 3 Nephi 27:28–29.

115. Enos 1:15.

116. D&C 132:40.

117. D&C 46:7.

118. See "Prayer," LDS Bible Dictionary.

119. See Bruce R. McConkie, *A New Witness for the Articles of Faith,* 379.

120. James 5:15.

121. Bruce R. McConkie, *A New Witness for the Articles of Faith,* 379.

122. See Moses 1:39.

123. Matthew 9:2–7, comments added.

124. James E. Talmage, *Articles of Faith,* 205.

125. Spencer W. Kimball, *Tragedy or Destiny,* devotional assembly at Brigham Young University, December 6, 1955.

126. See James 5:14–16.

127. John A. Widtsoe, *Evidences and Reconciliations*, 197, emphasis and comments added.

128. See D&C 49:6.

129. Joseph Fielding McConkie and Robert L. Millet, *Doctrinal Commentary on the Book of Mormon,* vol. 4, 41.

130. See Moses 1:9–10.

131. See Alma 15:5–11.

132. See Bruce R. McConkie, "Administrations," *Mormon Doctrine,* 21–22.

133. See D&C 128:8, 10.

134. See Mormon 9:25.

135. Gerald N. Lund, "Old Testament Types and Symbols," *Sperry Symposium,* 184–86.

136. Bruce R. McConkie, *A New Witness for the Articles of Faith,* 380.

137. D&C 90:24, comments added.

138. "Consecrate," *Merriam-Webster Dictionary.*

139. Bruce R. McConkie, *Doctrinal New Testament Commentary,* vol. 3, 273–74.

140. Bruce R. McConkie, "Consecration of Oil," *Mormon Doctrine,* 159.

141. See Bruce R. McConkie, "Administration," *Mormon Doctrine,* 22.

142. 2 Corinthians 13:1.

143. D&C 6:32.

144. Bruce R. McConkie, "Laying on of Hands," *A New Witness for the Articles of Faith,* 324.

145. "Laying On of Hands," *True to the Faith* (2004), 95.

146. See Bruce R. McConkie, "Administrations," *Mormon Doctrine,* 21–22.

147. "Administer," *American Heritage Dictionary.*

148. "Anoint," *American Heritage Dictionary.*

149. Spencer W. Kimball, "President Kimball Speaks Out on Administration to the Sick," *New Era,* October 1981, emphasis added.

150. "Oil, Consecrated," *Encyclopedia of Mormonism,* 1027.

151. Theodore M. Burton, *Conference Report,* April 1967, 42.

152. Gerald N. Lund, "Old Testament Types and Symbols," *Sperry Symposium,* 184–86, emphasis added.

153. Gerald N. Lund, *Jesus Christ, Key to the Plan of Salvation,* 61.

154. "Oil, Consecrated," *Encyclopedia of Mormonism,* 1027.

155. Jeffrey R. Holland, *Christ and the New Covenant: The Messianic Message of the Book of Mormon,* 163–64.

156. Spencer W. Kimball, "President Kimball Speaks Out on Administration to the Sick," *New Era,* October 1981.

157. Gerald N. Lund, "Old Testament Types and Symbols," *Sperry Symposium,* 184–86.

158. See D&C 110:13–16.

159. "Sealing," *Encyclopedia of Mormonism,* 1288.

160. Matthew 16:19.

161. Bruce R. McConkie, *Mormon Doctrine,* 615–16; emphasis added

162. Mark 8:22–25, comments added.

163. Spencer W. Kimball, "President Kimball Speaks Out on Administration to the Sick," *New Era,* October 1981.

164. 3 Nephi 17:7–8, emphasis added.

165. Alma 7:11–12.

166. "The Cleansing of a Leper," *Old Testament Student Manual,* 175–76.

167. Luke 18:22.

168. 2 Nephi 25:13.

169. Psalm 147:3.

170. James E. Faust, "He Healeth the Broken Heart," *Ensign* July 2005.

171. James E. Faust, "He Healeth the Broken Heart," *Ensign,* July 2005.

172. See "Grace," LDS Bible Dictionary.

173. See Moses 1:10.

174. David A. Bednar, "In the Strength of the Lord," *BYU—Idaho Devotional,* January 8, 2002.

175. 2 Nephi 25:23.

176. *Discourses of Brigham Young,* 163.

177. See Mark 12:41–44.

178. See Numbers 21:8–9.

179. See Clyde J. Williams, *The Teachings of Harold B. Lee,* 127.

180. Mark 9:24.

181. Job 13:15; 27:5.

182. Alma 36:27, emphasis added.

183. Luke 22:41–43, emphasis added.

184. James E. Talmage, *Articles of Faith,* 205.

185. D&C 121:1, 7.

186. See George Q. Cannon, *Journal of Discourses* 15, 379.

187. D&C 64:31–32.

188. D&C 88:73.

189. Neal A. Maxwell, "The Holy Ghost: Glorifying Christ," *Ensign,* July 2002.

190. D&C 88:68.

191. Joseph Smith, *Lectures on Faith,* 3:16.

192. D&C 98:1–3, emphasis added.

193. John 11:1, 3–4, emphasis added.

194. John 11:5.

195. John 11:34.

196. John 11:40, emphasis added.

197. John 11:43–45.

198. D&C 42:43.

199. Joseph F. Smith, *Gospel Doctrine,* 264.

200. Alma 38:4, emphasis added.
201. Matthew 10:7–8, emphasis and comments added.
202. Acts 3:3–8, emphasis added.
203. *Discourses of Brigham Young,* 335, emphasis added.
204. Bruce R. McConkie, "Patterns of Prayer," *Ensign,*
     May 1984.

SELECTED BIBLIOGRAPHY

American Heritage Dictionary, Cambridge, MA: Softkey International, 1994.

Hyrum L. Andrus and Helen Mae Andrus, comps., *They Knew the Prophet,* Salt Lake City: Bookcraft, 1974.

David A. Bednar, "In the Strength of the Lord," *Brigham Young University–Idaho Devotional,* January 8, 2002.

Rulon T. Burton, *We Believe: Doctrines and Principles of the Church of Jesus Christ of Latter-day Saints,* Salt Lake City: Tabernacle Books, 1994.

George Q. Cannon, comp., *Journal of Discourses,* Vol. 15, London: Latter-day Saints' Book Depot, 1854–86.

Church Handbook of Instructions, Book 2: Priesthood and Auxilliary Leaders, Section 1: Melchizedek Priesthood, Salt Lake City: The Church of Jesus Christ of Latter-day Saints, 1998.

Duties and Blessings of the Priesthood: Basic Manual for Priesthood Holders, Part A, Salt Lake City: The Church of Jesus Christ of Latter-day Saints, 1980.

History of The Church of Jesus Christ of Latter-day Saints, Vol. 4, Salt Lake City: Deseret Book, 1978.

Jeffrey R. Holland, *Christ and the New Covenant: The Messianic Message of the Book of Mormon,* Salt Lake City: Deseret Book, 1997.

Spencer W. Kimball, *Tragedy or Destiny,* a devotional assembly at Brigham Young University, December 6, 1955.

Connie Lamb and Gary P. Gillum, *BYU Speeches of the Year,* Provo, Utah: BYU Harold B. Lee Library, 1991. LDS Bible Dictionary, Salt Lake City: The Church of Jesus Christ of Latter-day Saints, 1979.

Gerald N. Lund, *Jesus Christ, Key to the Plan of Salvation,* Salt Lake City: Deseret Book, 1991.

——, "Old Testament Types and Symbols," *Sperry Symposium,* Salt Lake City: The Church of Jesus Christ of Latter-day Saints, 1979.

Bruce R. McConkie, *Encyclopedia of Mormonism,* New York City: Macmillan, 1992.

——, *A New Witness for the Articles of Faith,* Salt Lake City: Deseret Book, 1985.

——, *Doctrinal New Testament Commentary,* vol. 3 (Col. to Rev.), Salt Lake City: Bookcraft, 1973.

——, *Mormon Doctrine,* 2nd edition, Salt Lake City: Bookcraft, 1966.

Joseph Fielding McConkie, Robert L. Millet, and Brent L. Top, *Doctrinal Commentary on the Book of Mormon,* Vol. 4, Salt Lake City: Bookcraft, 1992.

Merriam-Webster Collegiate Dictionary, Springfield, MA: 2000.

Old Testament Student Manual, Salt Lake City: The Church of Jesus Christ of Latter-day Saints, 1980–81.

Joseph F. Smith, *Gospel Doctrine: Selections from the Sermons and Writings of Joseph F. Smith, Sixth President of the Church of Jesus Christ of Latter-day Saints,* Salt Lake City: Deseret Book, 1949.

Joseph Smith Jr., *Lectures on Faith,* American Fork, Utah: Covenant Communications, 2000.

James E. Talmage, *Articles of Faith,* Salt Lake City: Deseret Book Company, 1988.

True to the Faith: A Gospel Reference, Salt Lake City: The Church of Jesus Christ of Latter-day Saints, 2004.

Selected and Arranged by John A. Widtsoe, *Discourses of Brigham Young,* Salt Lake City: Deseret Book.

John A. Widtsoe, arranged by G. Homer Durham, *Evidences and Reconciliations,* Salt Lake City: Bookcraft, 1987.

Clyde J. Williams, ed., *The Teachings of Harold B. Lee: Eleventh President of the Church of Jesus Christ of Latter-day Saints,* Salt Lake City: Bookcraft, 1996.

ABOUT THE AUTHOR

Larry Barkdull is a longtime publisher and writer of books, music, art, and magazines. For many years, he owned Sonos Music Resources and published the Tabernacle Choir Performance Library. His published works have received a variety of awards: The American Family Literary Award; The Benjamin Franklin Book Award; and *Foreword Magazine's* GOLD Book of the Year Award for best fiction. His books have sold in excess of 250,000 copies and have been translated into Japanese, Korean, Italian, and Hebrew. Additionally, he is the creator and producer of the popular *Scripture Scouts* musical series to teach children the scriptures. He and his wife, Elizabeth, live in Orem, Utah, and are the parents of ten children and a growing number of grandchildren.

Larry Barkdull may be contacted through his website, www.larrybarkdull.com